C000001862

FALSEHOOD

After Hours Editions
New York ◆ Kingston
afterhourseditions.com

Front cover image: *Grand Union,* courtesy of Matt LaFleur
Cover design by Eric Amling
Typesetting by Guy Pettit
Editors: Sarah Jean Grimm & Eric Amling

Library of Congress Control Number: 2019917119

First edition
ISBN-978-1-7734082-0-2

After Hours Editions are distributed by Small Press Distribution

Printed on recycled acid-free paper

FALSEHOOD

emily brandt

AFTER
HRS
editions

"Reality is that which, when you don't believe it, doesn't go away."

Peter Viereck

Contents

i.

The only word

my father said was *error*
while flicking an unseen something off his wrist.

When he was a baby
my grams would rub his balls.

The back of my hand in vinegar
is what it's like to be born

to a pilot and a priestess in bed with Jesus.
Make of this blanket a steadying sail.

Mind of steel on the horizon. I am good forever.
I don't need your waterproof jumpsuit or your beer.

Why vomit in this wax-lined bag
when there is the sea? Talk Vietnam to me.

Time to go home

The sky is really
not-nice here is white
shit here and tight
in the shoulders in
the jaw. Turntable. Scan
for knots. Protect others
from this ego. Half
father hot mother. Playboy
attics in doctor closet.
Touch the slug I
dare you kiss it
lick the slug. Pocket
full of poison prescription
form. Church briefs. His
scissor eyes. Once I
define it they all
withdraw. I walk hard
to a place where
fingers reach through lawn
to skinny ankles gouge.

Careful what you wish under

It's one-point-four miles to get smokes at the station
  sells anything to anyone. A man
        behind jogs in his hand is his *careful.* Is it really?   Laugh
and then run

til POINT OF EXHAUSTION
        after just one.

Eight minutes to the woods
           still uncarved.
      Stab a knife
      in the trunk
      careful
      of a tree.

So much dirt in shoes, in beds
        of nails. So salt in hair. These scabs.
        Lift one up See slowly what's under.

Smoke outside the backdoor then a teacher outside walks to smoke
    get caught. Put quarters, six, in the slot of the bus take a seat
    share headphones with a boy older. He knows everything about the songs
    particularly the political ones. He is politic.

Pass ~~a car dealership, pizzeria, a state park,~~ colonial mansion, ~~an overpass,~~
      ~~an exit ramp, two diners, three~~ churches, ~~eleven nail salons, four~~
      ~~gas stations, twenty-two traffic lights, six bars, one ice-cream parlor,~~
      ~~steak~~house, ~~seafood market, two canals, a hospital, a KFC,~~

~~Taco Bell, McDonald's, Burger King, two Chinese restaurants,~~
~~one country club, dance studio, three law offices, a yarn shop, Y.~~

STRIP DOWN TO BUTTON-DOWN SHIRT AND BOXERS,
KNEE-SOCKS.

Pour cereal down the throat, turn over the ride.

The dial-tone dazes, hooks back the phone.
581-8579 cannot be
                                    fictionalized.

Stamp smokes out in attic. Garage. Basement. Front porch. Bedroom
windowsill. The shower.

   A needle and India ink: bored in rhyming meter.

To: you
are the greatest
kiss. Dream
my hands
           on your back
                           acne.

Look deep in the dog's beady eye.

Stand on a chair to reach higher shelf. Call a friend in fishnet stockings. Let's
   listen
           to the swish of corduroys
           lipstick's perfect purple lines
           veins visible through skin.

The squirrel skull in the woods, altar
of suburban cult. A head,
on the news, through the church
spiked fence.
Let's be girls
in the yard checking legs
and arms for ticks.

The Harbor

In this house, cancer. In this house arthritis, a severed limb,
hot wax. In this house, there's a cheater. In this house, travel low.
In this house, a body dull and steady as a rock. In this house,
a mother pulls mouse traps down from closet shelves, slaps a
child's hands like hoards of rodent feet. In this house, a man
girl-pulled her from bed and to the backseat of his car. In this
house, the Christmas bulbs stay up til Valentine's, a schism
in the rig. In this house, a dog that stings. In this house, the
shower's always cold. In this house, six boxes of fruit roll-ups in
a variety of flavors. In this house, watch the father. In this house,
everyone says their prayers. In this house, if given a choice. In
this house, there are spirits, unfriendly. In this house, an indoor
pool and two renters. In this house, a Chinese doctor and his
wife that no one's ever seen. In this house, the Missus called the
cops when a black man passed by, windows down and cricket
song. In this house, alabaster teeth and gingham breath. In this
house, heroin in a teenage vein. In these houses, cocaine. In
this house, there is a very small dog a very loud small dog. In
this house, the blinds match the carpet. In this house, everyone
belongs to a choir. In this house, a trampoline. In this house,
Jews. In this house, a very tan man eating an orange. In this
house, two sons are skinny and one son is fat. In this house, no
children are allowed. In this house, nails the length of spider
leaves and platinum hair. In this house, the lights are out on
Halloween. In this house, a priest comes for dinner. In this
house, a surge of electricity set fire but everyone survived. In this
house, a recluse who sits at her window, sometimes will wave.

Kills and cooks

Mama, she kills
and cooks meat in the pan.
*Some words shouldn't
be spoken – devil is one.*

The birds are terrible.
Their fat is a lie.
She can peel

back the skin
with her mouth
shut. *Whore
is the other.*

The wings
spread
before
the hammer
its blow
cool
and quiet.

Per annum

Roller skates tied together by laces strewn
over shoulder, drop. Pop in the tub.

Never bitch, said dad, *til you walk
in the Indian's moccasins*, ouch.

Soak still until Christmas then bust
the Santa myth, unlay auntie's veil

and illuminate, like the coils in the oven that sing
no singe the pig. Turn it up

with seafood seven kinds and Sambuca
for the kids. Then untimely

peel the "neighbor" drunk off driveway
forearm mopping tears, badging

some diagnosis on his breast then
wiping it clean.

Twelve

Inside the sea, water fills the body. Crossing
legs makes it harder to tread.

I never had a box of bracelets, a ballerina
twirling pink. Instead, a wooden box
with special things: news-clippings,

polyester rosebud, dogwood,
dog tag, stone, and Dolly's collar
for my neck. Here kitty
sweet-pea: five seven five – six one one eight.

Boys, they lie, while girls cry
wolf, and mother.

I quiver at the thought
of quaking earth, of salamander
birthing a monkey from its shell,

of forced consumption of tobacco
or cabbage-induced vomiting.

I collect gravity. It spreads out my skin
flat as dough, opens my palms. My hips
flatten under the weight.
There is comfort in ground
that does not move.

In a windowsill jar two plumeria stalks
form an X. Summer lizards eat flies
and shit wings which shimmer.

I pick green needles from tangled hair. Somewhere
mom listens to groceries fall in the back seat.

The Galley Bitch

Wake at 4 to be on time for my first job cutting
squid on the St. Anthony. The gulls in Captree State Park

are furious for fish and gas sheens the surface.
I am inspired by what's happening. Captain Bill

tells me I'll be pretty when I grow boobs
and hands me an ice-pick. The block of ice weighs

twenty pounds. I'll inspire my people too, show them
how to pull the spines from squid while smoking.

The mates already know this trick. They fidget
in the cabin with coffee and cards, wait for fish.

There's not any question about girls
being strong, about the open bay, about survival

at stake. I'd love to make some food for pay
but here everything's frozen, everyone drunk.

I hate one mate so I ash his burger. I fall
asleep in the galley and wake:

a blowfish bloats my pocket. I take his revenge lesson with me.

Exceptional

All the oysters in the sea
                    fit neat in this mouth

All the anything you want
            if you want bad
            enough

Shells drip   from her hair
            her wanting hair

                    this town is (all towns are) small

Giving head for a boat
            bound away   from want

I want to be brain surgeon   Ballerina   I want in the CIA

I want to be highway patrol   be national guard   Senator   To marry a senator

Full-time on-track   the Nation's Basketball Ass

I want to be Jeff Koons   Soluble   I want to be David Lynch

I want mansion   I want your company   To dive

All the oysters in the sea

        drive their wanting mouths
        seams the size of dinner plates

              make of my wanting   salable pearls

Girl claims her manhood

My three sisters shared the same walls
the same womb, the same wagon

swaying between screams: Walkman. Walkman.
Walkman. Fourth Walkman. Packed
extra batteries thank god, take me home.

I learned to use a blinker, to tailgate,
how to wipe the windshield, smoke out the window,
how to lock doors, how to open.

Purposeful at midnight. A round of shots before vomiting
into a hat took from someone's head, a stranger,
a bloodpunch and a phonecall, a door
and a quarter tank of gas.

This forged note to the nurse. Swollen
cheeks look like penance, but they're a concoction.
There are books about it, an encyclopedia. We ate
honeysuckles after the planes
flew by and sprayed.

Liminal dose

in this corridor   brush a coat
along white   wall   a stripe

of paint   shoulder bladed
forever a pulse   thudding

out crickets from the   wrists
and what else within   wanting   out

and what else within
wanting out   what words

some objects (here,
a list)   brushed acrylic

or with   butter
glisten gold expected like

a biscuit does not
expect a fist

or finger or a face
like a finger or a face

wants to find a hole
wanting out   what words

shoulder blade along
what walls and brush

acrylic gold what dark mood
hello now like a face

His sweet sixteen

was a lorrie
loaded full with coal.

Was a poplar
gold leaves wobbling.

A swallow
with swollen knuckles

vocal chords plucked
and restrung.

Hammers and gears didn't chide
in the wanted way
and the want grew
operatic and gastric.

Hair full
with cobwebs, maddening fingers
that picked and combed

on mother's couch, brushing names
and light in hair
swelling with storm.

The windowsill lined with horseflies,
his tiny dark legs
bent stiff toward the sun.

I stuffed my bra with socks

I say *I want to be her* but I know
I want to touch her.

I make myself
a mannequin.

The bee's stinger weaves
through blonde hair, traces map lines:

the way to the trail in the woods where the reeds
went up in flame, and to all the neighborhood pools,

which water is warmest
and which will sting your eyes.

Lunchtime conversation

Put the timer on for thirty minutes
and let's talk about something else.
The way the keys sound when you press them

but the strings are cut. Pulling
a clump of grass from the yard.
Don't pull the grass, Dad will yell.

I jumped off the top of the station wagon
and landed in the present moment.
Astrologically I shouldn't be here.

I should be in a different house with
a different sign. The old astronomers drew
the finest maps that were incorrect at a time

when people killed for ideas, which is now,
I folded a piece of paper over a comb
to make music and it worked. I froze a thread to

a cube of ice and it worked. I tried out math tricks
and they worked. I shoplifted and my skin worked.
I peeled open an orange and the smell came out. I flipped

over the handlebars, got strips of red roadburn
under my breasts and thought I would turn into a boy
and I did. It was easy. Any shirt would hurt

because of systemic friction. Like a tattoo coming off
over years. Every time your skin hits the surface
of the pool, there is rubbing. There are replacements

for what comes off skin but not for skin
itself, undervalued as the largest organ
despite common knowledge of the fact.

Moving the body is one nice thing about life. It's alarming
how skin separates you from the organs around you.
When I bake bread, the particles all stay in the pan

or so it looks, and so I believe. I simplified an equation
and it worked for a while. The first thought is not always
best, especially at a time when we are dying for thought.

There are different ways of liking football. You who like football
are extremely smart. Either way, it's nice to watch bodies move,
watch them work, and work ourselves sometimes too.

I have tried to like all bodies and failed. I favor the shape
of the bruise. Let's go back to talking work.
Let's talk the work that keeps the bread inside the pan.
Let's talk the work that keeps all those particles in their pan.

ii.

A *Man's World* is not just a saying

Everywhere I go I'm in a building
and every building was made by man
even the sidewalk, even the view. I saw
someone knit a kitchen once. It still looked

like a man. The fire belongs in the middle, and everyone
gathers round, plates full and knives sharp.
The buildings are so tall they hurt. Woman
didn't build the London Bridge that she made fall

a thousand times. When I ask Siri where I can
get an abortion, he tells me there are no abortion clinics
in New York City, and disguises his voice as a lady.
But when I ask Siri where to get my cock sucked she lists

escort services I never knew existed in my house.
Batter my heart, Siri. I never saw a man swoon
so hard as for your trinkets. I'd like to be a programmer
and create the next world: animals

everywhere, nonhuman. We call them dear
hold hands a little in the evenings and never ever
suck their milk or swipe their eggs. Just lay back
and look at nudey mags of The Farmer in the Dell.

Experiments with voice encoder

The air is incapable of holding anything
or the air holds multiple dimensions
as in acid trip, as in nightwalk.

All the people stayed home today despite the beautiful weather

and I watched from the front door as the mailman
walked by, his letterbag encased in a metal rolling device
for convenience, because some part of the system loves him
and respects his knees and his shoulders.

After work I stop playing, I just go straight to work again

on my art my pretty pictures my sound recordings
and leaf rubbings. I put all of the homemade instruments
on display and will tour them soon enough. Soon enough.

I pay my dues to my union and do math. They make three million dollars

per month and I wonder where everything went wrong.
At work, a man does something mediocre and we throw a parade.
We release our discordant voices into static and electrified air.
We empty the bedpans of our future selves. We are widows.

I pulled on some leggings today as a means of survival

and traveled to the back porch or the patio or lanai. The plants
are still dead like planets of another dimension.

If a woman kills plants, it symbolizes abortion.

Anything a woman does is shit compared to man.

I said that through the Vocoder and now I feel much better.
The vibrations are messing with somebody's Pacemaker.
The vibrations are messing with somebody's head
and the resulting rash itches as much as it burns.

If I swallow my money in the morning and you lift up my arms

at night, silver dollars will spill from my mouth
and the cocktail waitress will bring us free drinks,
red ones like I got in Reno. I saw wild horses on a hill.
They ran onto the road and over my car and onto
a rainbow and then the sky opened. They ran in.

I filled the story into a form where it said *last name*

and my credit report came back perfect. Top ten
in the country of fish fries and angel tattoos.
An angel tattoo is often a symbol for abortion
so next time you see one on someone
you'll know what to ask.

Slow movement towards gesture of goodwill to men in general

Disembodied beak in terminally ill
woman's hand marveling she
took it to her breast took it marred
to her lip this cartilage mouth
this trinket. A mouth of any animal
no matter which cannot
be a trinket yet there are diamonds
embroidered into paper on the walls
becoming audience to illness. The men
pressed the paper, hung
the paper with glue and everyone
stares. An ashtray not full
of ashes is how it feels to her hand
or how her hand perhaps feels in yours
as she clutches, as she razes.

Eyes Knees Groin Throat

I want to live in a body
that could hurt most other bodies.

I do not want to hurt other bodies. But my fist
could not break a wall
though I have tried.
I want to live with a wall-breaking fist.

I took a self-defense class a thing
some women do.
I am embarrassed
to say afterwards
I wanted the attack.

We entered one at a time
a large room. A woman cop
began directions. Said
You'll go up to this ATM
and a man attacked

threw me to the ground called me *Bitch*.
Another came. A cop too.
Mounted me and said
I'll rape you. And I punched and kneed.

I fought them off. They let me.
Their bodies were enormous, hard. And they get paid
each week to do this. I don't think about it much.

I like to think my body could be that large. I walk down
the street and pound the faces of the mermaids
and their delicious tails. I want to live in a body
that can swim across a channel. I want to fear myself
and never carry a gun. If I were born a cock
my father would have bit it off and taught me to do pull ups.
I would swell and swell. And perform well against a punching bag
until I got a girlfriend. I would stuff
the fist of my father into my ribcage
and grow a man around it.

Don't ask, tell

never said much said enough
never said half what he
never wanted to say a thing

was going to say *don't get caught*
was going to *your mother would*
was going to tell you *go*

tell me about bootcamp and war
tell me the showers and
occasional electrocutions

tell you the things you already
told me tell the forgotten things
forget and maybe the things
remember which aren't

A key tied to an ankle

A sign painted *dead whale*
isn't lying.

Take a closer look:
the water is filthymom

filthydad.
The water is filth.

Smells more like roadkill than fishgut
and no one carries a gun

not the cops or anyone.
This town eats sharks that swim

then sink like a stone at the mention
of your swingset disappearance

and reappearance as driver
of the all-girls' ice-cream truck.

We get to know each other
in strange ways these days.
Come over.

I've got nine Barbies and you can bring
Han Solo
and things will get good.
I might wet the bed

but a good friend would never. Would just
brush the crumbs from the sheets.

Folding sheets to stack neatly on the shelf

Hot wax applied to this love affair with money
Hair removal as commodity or otherwise uncouth

A whole house unfolds laundry as form of protest
People ransack drawers and closets support the piles

I'm sick of this inauthentic narrative voice
Would never recognize it on the dial up phone

I'm inclined to sand my lashes, look like the Book of Job
The terrors of God do set themselves in array against me

People can grow over the course of a moonrise but it's rare
Utterly narcissistic to think you can change anything

It took years to feel feelings and now I'm afraid
It took years to think thoughts and now I'm afraid

Terminal, with gesture of goodwill to men in general

There are airplanes wreathed into this carpet.

There is a crack in a windshield.

There is a man in a Pepsi shirt nodding his head.

A man carries a briefcase packed with puzzle pieces and nail polish.

     The initials RIP in decal.

     One leg crossed over another.

Swirls woven vortex into the ever-waiting carpet or hurricane.

Unending elevator ride.

Same sneakers for 15 years now and no end in sight.

     Sometimes fashion.

     Sometimes no.

Art and capital hit the windshield, say blam.

Left the phone in an elevator.

Calling it now.

Say it's time group three to board.

Groups one two three it's time.

I guess it's too late to live on the farm

This horizon line is twine held taut and I
am about to pluck, mistake it
for a Klonopin prescribed with magnesium
to still a dizzy head.
                              The injection was long
and warm between thighs.
                              Next time I was less
lucky and relied on herbs grown by my sister
turned to tincture with whiskeyed honey
in moonlight on my grandfather's land.
                              He dealt
guns.
        He raised ducks and women
plucked them featherless and warm, a few coins
in their pockets and trigger fingers.
                              They could
shoot the ducks off the horizon line sewn into
the seams of skirts worn working.
                              The seamstress'
steady hand was wife of a man, ate potatoes
wild and raw, a string connected across water
and whiskey black memory.
                              It's too late to live
on the farm which stands like a rifle surrounded
by houseframes bursting gadwalls and mallards.

This tincture really works when you take it
with Klonopin.

Before hurricanes the women
battened in broad and foreboding sun.

To kill

a duck thrust its head in this funnel and chop drain
repeat.

It's too late to live on the farm now
that the wind stopped and the tablecloths
have no tables holding their shapes.

It's easy to see the blades

when the fan is off.

It's easy to look straight at the sun
stark mind, set true on the trigger and nothing
much to hunt these days.

Accident involving imaginary men

What am I afraid of? a little rain never hurt no one. Slick
street bitch, stop this silliness. I am building a body
like Queequeg to be written by a dead man. I am going

outside. A little mud might kill you if you slip in it
twist yourself, starve in the woods where ticks like to dig.

None of this fear's worth the time it takes to walk
from here to the end of the driveway which is fifteen miles long.
Let's roll logs in the river instead, let's dance a little tonight.

About that, I love the woods, the green needles.
I saw about twenty frogs today and yesterday and every day.
At night, I'll drink shitty wine and listen to the screams outside.

I am not alone in this room anymore. I believe there is
someone here, hiding. I check the sheets, the drawers,
the blades of the fan, the edge of the carpet, behind the trees.

As an animal, I am separate from plants

Pulled ivy from the roses til my hands bled.
Picked clumps of fragrant basil, then refused it.
I am playing out a game with plants,
which ones die for nothing, which ones to eat.

This makes me master of a particular domain.
I experiment with master feelings.
They come easily.

The roses bloomed quick this year.
I pick and then discard them decoratively.
A skywriter struggles above and I laugh.
They let any man fly planes, any man spell.
Misshapen letters cloud the sun.

The shadows are illegible.
I am alone in this garden, rooted
to nothing. My arms do not tendril
against cement. I cannot pay them enough.
I pay for coolness and for shelter from the sun.

I am not mottled by most accounts.
My lungs and my skin are that of beasts but
I've been holding in this smoke for a century.
Come now to understand
the difference between scissors and shears.

Allow nothing to enter but the shapes of letters.

A salve as we recall all tools of manufacture.

The sound of the sound your mouth makes when a thorn sticks electric.

What I thought was vegetable is the cat

in the flowerbed, illiterate, about to scale.

A case for the control of guns in the hands of men

>>

You can't tell
who's in whose shoes
or what we am
when our first finger is triggered.

Miss Fashion wants
to be a MAN. She is (   ) a MAN!
She wants to bed the dragon.

Let's buy a squash blossom
from the pueblo:
die as HEADS of the Cult
of Appropriate Appropriation.

>>

O Sicily, come home to me
come whore to me
come with bones for me.
I carve o carve the bones
of my cousins
my brethren
a chandelier of bones
bright skeleton!

>>

Swing from the rafters:
O chariot O charisma
O P Q or rest your ex

your assault rifle registered
to the women of the world
united by guns in their purses
gum not guns.

Every day you die a tiny death.

> >

Every morning you are bored.
The light of the sun can't
stir you, with your
gun hanging out your body
shame shame! And don't you
want to shoot that thing!
Ready fire aim at chichi she!

Part your lips! Put your
hands on your hips! Let
the sun set. Let it settle.
Start to wriggle. Rest
your jaw. Your trigger
finger. Feel that. That's nice
right? Feel that. That's called
NICE.

I want to be the kind of man who smokes

with fingers like forktines stabbing at geodes, fruitless.
Down in the valley of discontent, a man

clubs his ball in the hole. A man kicks his ball
in the goal. A man throws his ball in the net.

Slow down the shock so it sounds
like lightning, a wheezing kettle, space heat.

A man runs his ball across the line hits out of the park.
A man bones his ball into the sun and it explodes

in an ecstasy of light. Two men volley
a ball back and forth, a midwinter tale. One man

victorious wears an item on his head, perhaps
a symbol, perhaps for smoke, for mineral light. The caves

are darker than ever before. Luminosity
is fruitless with all these fingers stabbing blindly

at anything dark, anything female. One no longer makes
paint from ground mineral, but buys. He pays cash and pours

the single color over the whole damn town. There is money
to be made, and lack-valleys full of pitch and holes.

Money on our knees

There is one fictional character I see
when I close my eyes and I want to
shoot him, which makes me a good reader.

One should use words like *elite* when loading
a gun. *Feminism* does not require severance
from the mother but needs a new non-binary construction.

Surveillance is less of a problem than it seems
until it becomes the worst imaginable crisis
of identity. I hate the sentence but I do love

how alligators go six months without eating.
I lay very still in the reeds. Being cold-blooded
is a challenge with identity. I dream of burying

a body in the desert. Actually the woods.
I'm in need of a shovel.   Mary's paint is peeling
and somewhere someone is buying or receiving

a brand new freshly painted beautiful resin Mary.
Someone is going to be blessed well. Sometimes
she paces around talking to herself. Sometimes she sings.

We're driving up the thruway to Woodstock
eyes closed. There's that body in the trunk and Mary's paint
is chipping where the passenger-side belt rubs

against her robes. She's a fine navigator
and she doesn't mind if I smoke, as long as
I keep the window cracked and the radio off.

It's only possible to drive in one direction even if we don't know
what direction is. There is no rattle in the trunk
where the shovel should be. North is not where the sun sets.

She prefers silence, which on the thruway means something
different. The car shakes like an airplane going west
or going south. Two different kinds of shaking.

How to

The only way left for a girl to be radical in America
is to camp in the woods for decades until she is ready to die

then build her own funeral pyre
surrounded by stones and light it well.

You are the genius of the ash heap and everyone
else in the woods, all of the scavengers, will mourn.

Safe space

I use my calm voice.
I use my calm voice with children.
I train to detach from emotion, exert power
in form of self-denial and denial of others
in form of resistance to softness
in form of military masculinity
that can erupt at any moment as rage.
I use my calm voice as it has been used unto me.

Search *how* Freud *researched* defenses.
When he studied defenses, he studied
men. Search *redirection* in place
of *control*. Men believe anything men say.
What other ideas are true?
I make a collage using my calm voice.
I tell a story using my calm voice.
In it, every single thing that is done is done by men
made by men
said by men
and every single one who is fucked is fucked by men.

I tell a story using my calm voice.
In it, Narcissus sees his reflection and statues
his head and his body and nobody cares
so the story drifts on a raft, sinks.
I tell a story using my calm voice.
In it, I project enough of everything for everyone.
Ego rests, resigns.
In it, we all walk on water, then synchronized dive.

Two kinds

Dream one:
a man stands
shirt collared
sky clear
sleeves crumpled.

Dream two:
a man stands
shirt collared
sky clear
sleeves pressed.

The consequence of a flag

The man is very smart, with bright eyes and chalky skin, straw hair cut short. His thesis is very smart. *We're fucked*, he says and I imagine him crop-topped. I think, *I'll know we're fucked when I see you in a crop-top*, and am unsure of how to take myself. My inability. My boy.

His thesis is *give up*. *We're fucked*. When he was small and played in dirt: *he's such a boy*, his mother said. When he put his unsure hand in hers, he was such a boy but no one said it. *He and she are fucked*, he says. *America can't keep us safe.*

I'll develop gills, I think. *I'll never wear a crop-top. I'm a boy*, I think. But I've yet to do violence to a body not mine. I've yet to wear my thesis so fearlessly on my tongue.

Thesis does not equal flag although they share a father. Department of. You wore that shirt two days ago. You must be fucked, or boy. *You should crop that top* is equal to, or less than, the violence done to bodies.

I note a scar on your right eyelid and think, *I have yet to*. I note a hole in your thesis which is equal to the violence of America can't keep us. *We're fucked*, he says to all his fathers. His right eye scarred with great intention.

I think how far I'll swim with my new gills. I note how small the shoreline flags will fade. My thesis will sound less than his when I speak it underwater, my intention greater than.

One or several silences in the girls' room at St. John's

Lights vibrate in the sky above my head
drop sky ceiling plastering down
and clumps of hair pulled as punishment
my god the things that teen boys do.

It's the sound of hovering
above a nest of one-ply fanning smoke
with one hand, the sound of
one door opening and steps,
the sound of about-to-get-raped
of *leave me be* of really no trouble
at all except that long and empty hall.

The smoke detector silenced
by her chewed up gum. *My god*
the girls' room heart and lung.

It's caught sound, the *You have no idea how bad
I need this* steps again and nothing but burning paper
again a slow sound and a sound reserved
for moments right before right now and after.

I'm about to quit. I'm about
to give up. I'm about to set fire. I'm about to practice
some scales. I'm about to hit water and this time
you won't hear my eyes shut

at the sound of unzip. It's the sound of unclench.

It's the sound of a fist balling. Of white
on white on white again. It's the sound of
pulsepulse. It's the sound of *I'm sorry.*
Of *so you know, you're not my girlfriend.*
It's the sound of my laugh. It's the sound of at you
the sound of the skin on the side of your face
or this desperate laughing. I can't hear
the sound of the other side. I can't hear

a blues song plays that pleases no one
and the sound is something like ca-ching

or a car engine dying. The sound of a body
washed. A female body as all bodies go
just like my sister just like my sister just like my sister.
The sound of paper wrapping tobacco. The sound
of encyclopedia pages turning. The sound of
he is the encyclopedia.

Man revises nature

All tents should be silk. I can't oil canvas
shoes anymore. I've had it. When I come
back to the city, everything is the same.
The men all wear beards again and the
girls are cutting their hair or braiding it.
Everyone is baking, especially the muscular ones.

Flowers are expensive for a reason.
All the lines radiate from the center.
We have a lot to learn as a species.
Our ancestors crossed very cold spaces.
If it were us, we would have surely died.
Everyone comes over and walks down
spiral steps. Sometimes someone ends up bleeding.

The piano hasn't been tuned for three years
but the man who tunes it has small hands
so we will be okay. Some strings go AWOL
and others march in line. I was in a bell choir
when I was a child. That nun could play
but couldn't sing. Me neither. Many nuns
have survived violent fathers.

Boys like to stick with other boys and girls
like to stick with girls until that stops. Girls like
to be the only girl in the room more or less
than boys like to be the only boy. These truths
are harmful to certain kids. I never wanted

to be a girl, but not for the reasons you think.
Boys were allowed to bike ride with their shirts off.

My husband is really good at doing flips.
Like seriously good at this. It makes me very
nervous. The tension of the diving board.
And the little ones say *Wow*. There is
an inflatable shark on the loose. And only
one raft, not big enough for us all. Soon,
the pool guys will come and find us bleached here.

The pool guys are always guys. I don't know
if their work is skilled or unskilled labor.
I've never had a pool. I lied to colleagues
in an icebreaker and said I know
how to tune pianos. And when asked what tools
I used, I said an awl and a really good ear. People
who don't know awls believed me and I won that game easily.

We were in a townhouse. We
were in a gilt gold frame. My grandfather left
an abalone table and a statue of some princess.
The carved legs were wobbly, and everything
collapsed in the middle of a night. Plaster dust
all over. There were no survivors.

My grandpa loved ornate things, a man of taste.
Men are always reinventing taste. When I found
my tastebuds for the first time, I thought
I was dying. Maybe kids will start growing
teeth from their throats. We agree
that something has to change.

iii.

The sword that severs all

If marriage is an oak and satin tomb.

If marriage is a man involved with state.

I am swimming naked and the lake is very cold.

If the absence of a part necessitates a woman.

Play Fuck-Marry-Kill.

The outcome obvious and false.

/ /

I slink around inside a wall.

I'm captain of the ship. I'm commander.

If a part necessitates a male.

A genital that shapes precise.

If a female shapes female.

A signature more persuasive than a stamp.

If rough shape can rule multitudes of definition.

/ /

If I practice perfect your signature I am now you.

If I practice my signature perfect, the law.

If a part can enter a body, whose?

A genital shaped like an unlike genital so

who? The definition legally established:

Undo your uterus and undo your breasts.

/ /

Each of my breasts was engaged.

Each is married. My uterus married.

My two arms and hamstrings. My fingerprints.

Each of your hamstrings is mine now.

Your two arms and testes. Your fingerprints.

The state in its wisdom.

I'll curl into you each night.

There will be nights I don't.

/ /

If a signature can break when someone is inside.

The permutations of a shape made visible.

Kill this him before he kills me.

Marry that him because he probably won't kill me.

A sword lies between us. I wish on its stillness

to end the shape of our laws.

/ /

If I do anything but swim, I'm out of line.

If naked swimming will you fuck?

If bathing suited will you marry?

Things change shape beneath the water.

If swimming out of shape would kill.

The laws are fewer in the sea than in this lake.

Everyone wants to wear the resistance

What sound do
stars make
do they sound
like they're burning
do they say
the name of
their wife? What
is this galaxy
and who decides?

The pine trees
fatten at dark.
The wind as used
in German poetry.
Now do you
trust? Nothing can
matter but oil
in my skin
the same elements
as my ancestors.

I want to
connect with my
blunder. Darkness is
comfort disguised as
alarm. An encircling
expansive full sound.
Some kind of
stiff blazing girdle.

Emily

Well, it's time for sleep again, bang
the pillow to my head.

I'll call you three times in the morning
 send you sweet texts all day. Fill my thermos
with spiced tea. I'm here in the mirror

    just giving and giving. Slide

down your pants, the pillow.

    Brush the greens out of my teeth.

*

A bathroom in Natalie's old house
    sitting, both, tubbed.

June gulls flock.
            The window squawks.

*

Emileeeeeee
            we're going to lift you up

we're going
        to lift you
    up. You're light
as
                a feather.

*

Why does Augustine

                confess

        to me?

*

May I become more free, more still,

        go beyond language

into heart failure,

        get back
to the back of the brain
    turn the microphone on.

*

I like how you can look

　　at 9 x 9 and know

81!
　　　and never say the numbers

in your head.

*

　　Shadow work.

*

　　　　Gather around
the white table. Aunt Betty's old thing.
It's so close to the stove.
Who set up the American kitchen
so we have to carry our food
　　　　from fire to table?
A real problem

like the locks on the door

　　　　keeping me in and you all out.

Well, I'm disappointed

　　　　　　by this:

Immigrant fragment

Fifty miles from here / a townhouse boy salted and packed

with cousins on Ellery / Sicilians like bricks / Migration as planting

seeds in the soil cement poured on top / A lifetime / and wife /

then scattering

but I don't even know any names of those kin / A procession /

new status as white

a pouring / a flight / or vocation / to assimilate is to erode / then return /

with a plan

to destroy by amnesia / call it success / A razing / This marriage / its status /

a scorpion

in the bedsheets and a percolator on repeat / the hollowing between ribs /

a directed

explosion / no structure to rest under / or inside of / To rest is to ruin /

on purpose

Till death

Today I went insane in the shower, shaved
everything. I'd rather sit in a parked car in a heat wave.

I have a husband. I never had that before.

If sitting in a hot car in a heat wave
I must now consider how he might feel
and he might be concerned.

I don't want to be
a husband's concern.

Taking up space

I sharpen my nails on the hard sand of Thebes.

I position a black bow between my shoulders.

I invite birds to roost in my hair, peck seeds.

I pluck the color from glass, release thistles.

I ignore water and land, fill my palette with fire.

I confuse Philomene with Philomel while filling my urn.

I flatiron and can't feel my breasts with these hands.

I accept your invitation to skin my nose.

I see clearly to our other side and it stuns.

I weave a world of rainbow armor.

I declare myself and the hour turns violet.

I want to merge into eternity with your bountiful bountiful light

There is nothing for me to do. Each wave is a hurricane.
I dive in. I go to sleep. A hollow roll of water. Saline.
My eyes are comforted here. I need, I don't need.
So much water I am vomiting and that is when I know
you, there silhouetted in front of the sun—
the massiveness swelling my heart now. You see.

Wind and waterfall are twins, wind older by many minutes.
Start coming upon or making me come. I want my twin back—
where is she? Busting open all the rainsticks with our hearty legs,
our quad-skin welted pretty now and heavily blessed.

I told you to stop, you did, and I told you to start
and you did and I fled and ignited a trail behind
of all the people on our street holding hands
and even the police, singing. I change my mind.

Sleeptalking to a married man

You noise me awake and the sheets are sliding off the bed, polyester blanket, a bull's eye. Sound rides up the side of the building from the street through glass. There is a tap dripping some liquid melting. There is motion we can hear.

We each dream a crowd of people and so there are crowds in the room with us and some of them speak and the speech is slow enough to hear. It's maybe a girl I met or a girl you slept with when you were young enough to make love without speaking.

When each crowd speaks, he puppets your mouth or mine and so we each become a stadium of people of this country and of other countries too, and just as we can watch sport in other languages and understand narration through gesture, we can understand words and sounds that are not words, come out through our mouths and through the pores in our arms and shoulders and sometimes the sound that grows out of the hairs on our heads and on our sex.

I couldn't remember any word except the feeling of money being blown up through the grates on the street, up high enough to fly outside the window and how we watched it fly but never opened the thin curtain. Shadows of great moths with fat bodies that we did not care for. The shadows of bills like confetti falling up and filling the pockets of a cranky god in space. Every concept is a human concept. Neither the bills nor the god make sounds loud enough to drown out the sound of your crowd and my crowd of people barely breathing underneath our skins.

iv.

Secret garden

Stock up on caffeine wander on a floor look to former notes from former self from friend revise revise rewrite revise and still it looks exactly the same as your grandmother's Alzheimer's scribble / her voice once recorded on a handheld device with no playback potential.

There are methods for recording that can structure your thoughts as digital or analog codes.

Can "secret garden" refer to anything
other than genitals?

Some might say that "analog codes" is a misnomer and thereby sever the contract by which this structure is standing.

I woke up in a pool of water each day for a month and very few things changed.

I embellish my statement again and again and very few things change.

I draw parallels between this and that (pronouns replacing injustices too painful to speak of).

I seek to sacrifice the "I" which truly is not possible and so my sacrifice goes unacknowledged by the gods.

Late this afternoon I break the net around clementines.

There are maybe fourteen or sixteen clementines inside. Maybe twenty.

I bought these solely for the purpose of experiencing breaking open the net.

I do not like fruit. I like the smell so much I find the key.

If it says add three cups of Epsom salt, I surely need four.
The term ally applies most aptly to magnesium.
After soaking   my thirst is desert deep / A thirst that shatters.

I understand the power of hydration, but not the purpose. Why does solid body need so much liquid and don't say we are 70% because that's a schoolboy lie.

There's no other way to say what's next in this nonfictional mythology:
A man rapes a woman.

A first draft reads: a man rapes a woman and nothing happens to him.
Nothing! happens to him.

A revision reads: what happens to a man after he rapes a woman?

A revision replaces "rapes" with "sexually assaults." A headline rewrites
"has sex with."

I know what happens to a woman. At least three hundred versions of I know. It's not hyperbole. I can share a hyperlink.

Omit previous unreadable pages. Boil a pot of water for dinner. Search "recipe" and be utterly overwhelmed.

Get the combination of chemicals wrong and everything glacial*. See the term *comes crashing down.

Here a hologram
A sea of ivy
Lift your head
No no tuck it
No no I
have
a

car

comes with certain privilege
including freedom, a radio antennae.

v.

In the poem "JOANNE," Joanne Kyger says "Well I just want you to / know the truth."

To POEM is to say YOU as in *all* of you, to say ECHO as in I, or

CONFESSION, to say UNIVERSE. Awoke today to think:

I attempt honesty and artistry. The harmony and conflict between the two frightens.

ARTISTRY, this strange label, this purpose so deeply inside of utility that it's outside.

Momentary disembowelment in gilt frame consumed with side of greens.

I am trying hard to listen to thoughts instead of to generate thoughts.

Someone who knows said that after reading a haiku, for one moment, you experience god.

I am not sure about god or haiku but this idea rattles around and I am listening.

Later Kyger says, "It's always free / It's always easy."

Rejection of Adam's body

>>>

Upper back a chestnut tree / but everything else
loose or fixation. A thump / in the hubcap. An underwater
light fixture. No Adam no Adam not / the black pickup,
the lumber planks, small dog, boat motor,
up and down the sound of water / washing. What will you do?
        Be bathed with slack jaw
        to let air pass through body.
        Bone-thief, be a reed.
Strap / your shoes down and lift
the rest. What useless shifts what / not time. To run up road
and finally breathe. Everyone holds pain / in hand hip ankle and we need
all the help we can get. Most feet are exposed
but mine I hid. I forget / what I'm supposed to do.

>>>

How drone to sleep / we molasses in daytime
stirring coffee cold in largest oven wear / chickens run
something old in the water / animal love in the house bed flowers
tell me / breast and bones and fat skin flesh butter
oil lamp trained by gum smacks and vodka soda hey here's a story for you
        ((or gum smacks and hey here for you a vodka soda))
all the other times I was over there with someone else watching /
handsome eaters
who never question rule of law the word our father and their fathers
stop / for these bodies do not look like theirs

> > >

Heavy lidded in a grotto full with sound and shit / help me iron fold and wash
I can't wait to give up job to keep the door wide for others / too many lions,
feel me?
too much Adam / tell me something new today tell me the chicken that some
old woman
will eat with her man who will pick his teeth with its bones
and lubricate with its fat and take the cells of its flesh and make them his
Tell me about the chicken and this man and woman / Identify them first /
by name
Walk this path hey please not angry just talk / what is the worst thing
without rage
you can say to an offspring? / Pour another glass my head is foggy and I'm
falling asleep where
is Monica she got so thin and her hair so dark I love to touch / Keep the bone
in the jamb
of the basement I don't want love / of what is this insane meadow / where can
my house rebuild / with view of things unnamed

FALSE! DISGUSTING!

after Donald Trump & Jeffery Epstein Rape Lawsuit and Affidavits

1. Who is passive (*Plaintiff* was subject to*)? Who active (*Plaintiff*)
   brings this action against*)?)
)

2. And upon what? the table of the catered feast? the bed made for)
   the purpose?)
   Upon information)
   and belief)
   inter alia.)
)

3. At what point can (or does) one* consent)
   to a *savage* (in this case: *powerful. wealthy. man.*)?)
)

4. One condition of *incapable*)
   under New York law)
   is the existence of childhood, a child cannot, and yet)
   it's alleged)
)

5. there were *similarly situated*)
   minor females*.)
)

6. *Plaintiff* was* (like all good stories) *by promises* (I* too received)
   these) *enticed* .)
)

7. The promises (   ) vanish as *proximate result*)
   of the sexual a******s and r***s)
   (inter alia) *perpetrated by the Defendants*)
   (savages, promisers) *upon her*.*)

8. Another female* declares *I* personally witnessed*   )
    Plaintiff* has suffered   )
    Plaintiff* has been subjected to   )
)
9. And this phrase,   )
    disappear like Maria*,   )
    repeated.   )
    Disappear. Like Maria   )

*The Equal Rights Amendment, introduced in 1923, declares: "Equality of rights under the law shall not be denied or abridged by the United States or by any State on account of sex."**

**To date, amendment has not been ratified.

Attachment

What seems random
is geometric precision.
A pattern in a carpet.
A car engine. Infinite
mother love. A turbine.
Here, a stream
and the water is
perpetually clear.
Is perpetual. Is
perpetrating. Is
purposed. A proposal.
A sniffle or something
strawberry. Or Cola.
An elephant in a turnstile.
A sabotage. A sneeze.
A liminal space. I was
always on the doorstep
of unworthy. A challenge
of gender. Hermaphroditic—
does it count that I feel
like this? Can I invent
an origin story of myself
my genital? Or is that one
I don't get
to write? My mother
collected my birth
on a typewriter. It's in
a flat box on the shelf

of a closet. A comforter.
A sleeping bag. A crinoline
skirt to hide in. Fence slats.
Marshmallow in a jar. A touch
of nasturtium. Nostalgia.
A pumpkin aioli. A shredded head
of lettuce. A lucky charm
and a home on this range
this cul-de-sac, this unopened
envelope, this trove. A fire
set by a pirate to lure. A field
full of men and one woman's
legs. Can I write her
origin story? What is she
called? What can she
possibly be called?

I need rich, low maintenance friends

Tile white, believing: hygiene
but the door stays closed.

Why not build a bath of bricks or glass, or twig
this pipe from drain to sea.

The water-sound run underground
colored by our chemical peel, our skin
elastic shed in taffy strips, runs like honey, down.

What else to marvel but bathroom style
modernity and leisure time. How exactly my lineage
did bathe? What river, bucketbasin, frequency and duration.

What evidence of their cleanliness
to their public they'd present?

An everyfamily remodels
bathroom shinier, works a hundred
hours funding toilet
fixtures, maybe tub and tile

upgrade to keep the look contemporary
shit-free clean. Our ancestors
bathed and emptied by wick and fire,
by light of the sun, its agents. I go

many weeks without a flame in any form.
My plants line my sill
and eat sunlight.
I commend them.

Never gonna dance again

What is he saying about priests and preachers? Can I pick just one corruption to drill my teeth against? I got a body like you. I experiment with shaving and not, with cutting hair and nail then letting things that grow grow, and relish the primary implication of each cut.

I pall behind the pulpit. Pale under the influence. Punk what power I've been given. My dad raged about *Push 1 for Spanish* and who needs to learn what. I too have thoughts on this, my father with the red rage patriarchy that gave me half of my genetic heft, half my ribcage and its ability to stick where it's supposed to

like those campaign stickers on scuffed-up bumpers. Our national treasure is 65 million listed versions of she failed how. Those shoulders wide as the doorframe and won't get stuck no never.

I wanted an elephant with her trunk raised in an S

an alphabet of gesture evolving sans ivory.

I wanted something sacred unmarked by man.

This requires real work and tearful apologies to slip into this glimmer of want, of wanting to cry mostly because when you're crying you can't start to cry.

Somewhere there is something good worth holding on to on to on

/ / /

God now we produce our own guilty feet in a variety of forms now
and God now is the time to give us the power to rain ourselves only if we
want to
and decide the symbolic meaning of the rain now Sir.

/ / /

Filled a muffin tin with cracked quartz and blood from my hands and
there is enough to feed everyone here. A range
a range around us there was once a rhythm here, a logic.

/ / /

The night robs light the light robs dreams the cat stretches in his bed a nest of
his own hair
the cat an orphan the cat a survivor the cat seeks refuge the cat a plaything
the cat an object the cat a pet. What is a pet something to pet in the night
something to rob?

/ / /

Three roundish roaches scurry the sink. Something breaks the roof three
stories up.

Maybe a tree almond or drone

now

that

you're

gone

vacuum
the backs of the drawers with ferocity. Put my body
in the streets.

Walled in, watching people mowed down by motorists with loud muscles and
slobbering.

Sipping gin waiting for the executions to begin.

Everything outside is replicated within

To start this is to fail immediately and yet to persist.
Steam rises from black tea as if no time has passed as if
this landscape is the landscape from which its leaves were pulled.

Upon waking I make a rough attempt to shift my weight into my hands
as if the boundaries of my species are illusion
as if by will alone I could tumble up instead of fall.

Each desire pushes outward through symptomatic movement.
The snow outweighs my car, accumulates height and will.
After a long time outside looking, I open my eyes.

Inside, a self-made man solders over a cutting board
culled from a landscape of strip-searched oaks.
The universe has not yet opened so I note that I am not the center of
mythology.

Steam still parts my lips to welcome the burn of boiled water.
What wisdom is this that scorches the throat
binds my hand to the kettle and dollar.

I shower today then immediately clean the glass
to leave not a trace of my clean nor my dirty.
The reflection of a reupholstered couch holds its shape.

In this house, only some leaves grow toward the light.
I question the source. Scour the want ads. I burn my mouth again
and again until blisters appear and I burn the blisters.

Undoubtedly I treat others the many ways the world treats me.
I hang my head out the window and melt snow on the trap of my tongue.
Note the politics of action taken by my body, its identifiers.

Note the spiritual implications. Note good timing for my blistering mouth.
Publish these notes on your community billboard and note who is standing
still in the schoolyard and note who has died, and how.

The news lies about the way that bodies move, about the weather.
The sun slides behind some pornographic trees. They catcall.

Acknowledgements

I'm grateful to the editors of the following journals, in which poems in this collection appeared, sometimes in different form:

> *92Y Words We Live In*, *Apogee*, *Bodega*, *Coconut*, *Deluge*, *Dream Pop Press*, *Emotive Fruition*, *Gigantic Sequins*, *jdbrecords*, *Jellyfish*, *Leveler*, *Literary Hub*, *Lyre Lyre*, *phantom*, *Poor Claudia*, *Print-Oriented Bastards*, *Sink Review*, *Tammy*, *The Atlas Review*, *The Feeling is Mutual*, *The Mackinac*, *The Offing*, *The Portable Boog Reader*, *The Recluse*, *Tirage Monthly*, *TRNSFR*, *Washington Square Review*, *Women Poets Wearing Sweatpants*, *Wreck Park*

Earlier versions of some of the poems in this collection appeared in the chapbooks *Behind Teeth* (Recreation League, 2014), *ManWorld* (dancing girl press, 2015), and *Sleeptalk Or Not At All* (Horse Less Press, 2015). I have so much gratitude for Kristy Bowen, Matt L. Rohrer, and Jen Tynes.

"Experiments with Voice Encoder" is published in *Brooklyn Poets Anthology* (Brooklyn Arts Press, 2017). Thank you to Jason Koo and Joe Pan.
A related poetry film is featured at Alina Gregorian's "The Reading Series" blog at *The Huffington Post*. Thank you Alina!

I'm particularly grateful to the support of Poets House, and all of the 2016 fellows, and Saltonstall Arts Colony.

Thank you to all of the poets, artists and loved ones who offered inspiration, teachings, collaborations, insights, and friendship: particularly to Haoyan of America, Sini Anderson, Anne Carson, Chia-Lun Chang, Marisa Crawford, Steven Cramer, Alex Cuff, Bob Currie, Iris Cushing, Joey De Jesus, Thomas Dooley, r. erica doyle, Natalie Eilbert, Ryan Evans, Adam Fitzgerald, t'ai freedom ford, Sarah Glidden, Nicole Göksel, Katya Grokhovsky, Julia Guez, Edward Hirsch, Jen Hyde, Steven Karl, Yusef Komunyakaa, Deborah Landau, Nicole Lanzillotto, Amy Lawless, Natalie Lessing, Monica McClure, Jennifer Nelson, JoAnna Novak, Meghan O'Rourke, Sharon Olds, Leila Ortiz, Morgan Parker, Ali Power, Kristen Prevallet, Emily Raw, Matthew Rohrer, Melissa Shaw, Bianca Stone, Kiely Sweatt, Paige Taggart, Julia Wey-Burgoyne, Rachel Zucker, and so many more.

Thank you Cynthia Manick and Sara Jane Stoner for the nurturing help shaping this collection.

Tremendous gratitude to Eric Amling and Sarah Jean Grimm for making it all happen, and happen beautifully.

Thank you: Ma, Dad, Maria, Laura, Julia, Rani, William, Jason, Max & Bear, and all the rest of my family, blood and chosen, and to the ancestors.
Adoration to Rio (RIP) and Gnocchi.
Infinite love to Eric Pitra and your magical mind.

Emily Brandt is a poet of Sicilian, Polish & Ukranian descent, born and raised on Long Island. She's the author of three chapbooks, a co-founding editor of *No, Dear*, curator of the LINEAGE reading series at Wendy's Subway, and an Instructional Coach at a NYC public school. She earned her BA in Psychology, English, and Women's Studies from Boston University, her M.Ed from Pace University, and an MFA from New York University, where she facilitated the Veterans Writing Workshop. She lives in Brooklyn with her love, and their dog, Gnocchi.